The Little Book of Dog Quotes

The Little Book of Dog Quotes
Published by
Barzipan Publishing
www.barzipan.com

© Aubrey Malone 2018

2 4 6 8 9 7 5 3 1

ISBN 978-1-9997633-4-3
Kindle edition ISBN 978-1-9997633-5-0

Printed and bound by Interak Printing House, Poland

The Little Book of Dog Quotes

Aubrey Malone
with illustrations by Richard Jolley

Barzipan
Publishing
not what you'd expect

To Deezer

We'd had dogs before but Deezer was the first dog who was all mine. A cross between a pointer and a sheepdog, the first time I saw him he was tied to a kennel by a rope so tight it seemed to be squeezing the life out of him.

He was skin and bone, and we bought him from his cruel owner. When we got him home, he jumped up on the table and ate six lamb chops. That made us love him all the more.

We were inseparable until my first year at university, during which I went to London to be a barman for the summer. When I came home Deezer was gone. He'd bitten a young girl under the eye in play and had to be put down. My parents hadn't told me they were putting him down because they knew I wouldn't have it. I knew why they had to do it but my heart was broken. He was such a gentle dog. I used to think of him being in dog heaven like Old Shep from Elvis Presley's song. 'If dogs have a heaven,' Elvis sang, 'there's one thing I know, Old Shep has a wonderful home.'

Aubrey Malone

CONTENTS

Chilterns Dog Rescue Society would like to thank Aubrey and Medina Publishing for putting together this wonderful book of dog quotes. We are a small independent charity which takes dogs with nowhere else to go.

Life in a Rescue Centre can be a serious business but we have had our fair share of funny moments, many of which we are reminded of when we read this book! The reason we work so hard rescuing, rehabilitating and rehoming dogs is because of the unconditional love that they give in return. Our lives are enriched by their presence. The wagging tails when you walk in the door, the reason to get outside and appreciate our surroundings, the comfort they provide during the sad times and the fun we have during play times – they truly are man's best friend.

Stephanie Strong
Chilterns Dog Rescue Society

Man's Best Friend

When a man's best friend is his dog, the dog has a problem.

Edward Abbey

If your home burns down on you, rescue the dogs. At least they'll be faithful to you.

Lee Marvin

They say, 'If you want a friend, buy a dog.' But I don't need to. I have Barbara.

George Bush Sr

If diamonds are a girl's best friend and a dog is a man's best friend, what chance do man-woman relationships have?

Cynthia Heimel

They say a dog is a man's best friend. I don't know. How many of your friends have you neutered?

Larry Reeb

My dog was my only friend. I told my wife I needed more than one. She bought me another dog.

Henny Youngman

I've heard that a dog is a man's best friend. That explains where men are getting their hygiene tips.

Kelly Maguire

Dogs may be our friends but they won't pick you up at the airport.

Bobcat Goldthwait

A dog who thinks he's man's best friend has obviously never met a tax lawyer.

Fran Lebowitz

Outside a book a dog is a man's best friend. Inside a book it's too hard to read.

Groucho Marx

I once had a dog who actually believed he was man's best friend. He kept trying to borrow money from me.

Gene Perret

My dog is my soulmate. We both take naps by the fire, we both eat when we feel like it, we both hate the vacuum cleaner.

Elayne Boosler

You can laugh at a dog but not at a cat. Dogs don't mind because they want to be pals with you. Cat's don't.

Ernest Hemingway

Dogma, Doggerel and Dog Philosophy

Dogs aren't our whole life but they make our lives whole.

Roger Cains

One reason a dog can be such a comfort when you're feeling blue is that he doesn't try to find out why.

Elizabeth Taylor

My dog is an existential retriever. He brings back everything I throw but he's not sure why.

Dave Allen

If your dog won't come to you after having looked you in the face, go home and examine your conscience.

Woodrow Wilson

To call Richard Brautigan's poetry doggerel is an insult to dogs.

Lazlo Coakley

Don't accept your dog's admiration as exclusive evidence that you're wonderful.

Ann Landers

Dogs are co-dependent. Cats are independent. We humans hover somewhere in between.

Charlie Quackenbush

Dogs made a pact with mankind about 10,000 years ago to do anything we want. As a matter of honour we should reciprocate.

Orson Welles

We don't own our dogs. Our dogs own us.

Dodie Smith

You need a licence to buy a dog or drive a car but they'll let any jackass be a father.

Martin Abbott

My dog died when he knew I was going to be able to make it on my own.

Mickey Rourke

Man is a dog's ideal of what God should be.

André Malraux

He who lives among dogs must learn to pant.

Fred Hoyle

Dogs have better manners than the British. At least they greet each other.

Katharine Hammett

Owning a dog may be the only opportunity a human ever has to choose a relative.

Wyatt Johnson

If you eliminate smoking and gambling you'll be amazed to find that almost all of an Englishman's pleasures are mostly shared by his dog.

George Bernard Shaw

A dog's saliva can mend a broken heart.

Jennifer Neal

Pavlov's experiments with dogs were were the salivation of psychology.

John Crosbie

The truth is, Pavlov's dog trained Pavlov to ring his bell just before he salivated.

George Carlin

Anyone who doesn't know what soap tastes like never washed a dog.

Franklin P. Jones

Dogs are wise. Unlike humans, they crawl away into a quiet corner to lick their wounds. They don't rejoin the world until they're whole once more.

Agatha Christie

It's dog eat dog in this rat race.

John Deacon

Politics is a dog's life without a dog's decencies.

Rudyard Kipling

Dogs are better than human beings because they know but do not tell.

Emily Dickinson

The average dog is a nicer person than the average person.

Andrew Rooney

Tolerably early in life I discovered that one of the unpardonable sins in the eyes of most people is for a man to go about unlabelled. The world regards such a person as the police do an unmuzzled dog.

Thomas Huxley

A dog's philosophy of life is that if you stare at someone long enough, they'll eventually give in.

Mark Twain

You don't need a guide dog for hindsight.

David Blunkett

Pat a dog and you'll have a job forever.

Benjamin Franklin

Don't sweat the petty things. And don't pet the sweaty things.

George Carlin

I am fond of pigs. Dogs look up to us and cats look down on us but pigs treat us as equals.

Winston Churchill

When a dog is drowning, everyone offers him water.

Proverb

If I have any belief about immortality it is that certain dogs I have known will go to heaven, and very few people.

James Thurber

To sit with a dog on a hillside on a glorious afternoon is to be back in Eden.

Milan Kundera

My husband converted to Catholicism only after he'd been assured dogs could enter heaven.

Mary Wesley

Lending money to a spendthrift is a bit like pelting a trespassing dog with meat dumplings.

Chinese proverb

Life is unpredictable. Some days you're the dog, some days you're the fire hydrant.

Dwight Hogarth

Dogs are more interesting than women because they don't know they're gorgeous.

Hal Roach

I've seen a look in dogs' eyes, a quickly vanishing look of amazed contempt that tells me they basically think humans are nuts.

John Steinbeck

If you try to run over a dog on a bicycle he knows how to avoid you but if you try to miss him he doesn't.

Mark Twain

Happiness to a dog is what lies on the other side of a door.

Charleton Ogburn

Did you ever walk into a room and forget why? I think that's how dogs spend their whole lives.

Sue Murphy

A door is what a dog is permanently on the wrong side of.

Ogden Nash

To his dog, every man is Napoleon. Hence the constant popularity of dogs.

Aldous Huxley

There are enough people in the world. I did my part by raising dogs.

Anita Day

Why is that, when the doorbell rings, the dog always thinks it's for him?

Noel V. Ginnity

Barking Mad

Every time I go near the stove my dog barks. He knows I'm a lousy cook.

Phyllis Diller

When your child is locked in the bathroom with water running and he says he's doing nothing but the dog is barking, call 911.

Erma Bombeck

Barking dogs don't bite but they themselves don't know that.

Sholem Aleichem

I don't get any respect from my dog. He barks at the front door every time I'm about to go out. I think he wants me to leave.

Rodney Dangerfield

Best in Breed

I've got a Chihuahua. They're very small. If you lose one, just empty your purse out. He might be in there.

Joe Carroll

I'm the only boxer in my family. The rest of us are Alsatians.

Barry McGuigan

Dachsunds are ideal dogs for small children because they're already stretched to such a length the child can't do much harm to them.

Robert Benchley

I was the youngest of five boys. My father bought us a dachshund so we could all pet him at the same time.

Bob Hope

Russian dogs are the fastest in the world. They have to be – the trees are very far apart.

George Burns

A Pekingese is not a pet dog. He is an under-sized lion.

A.A. Milne

Dachshunds have to wag their tails by remote control.

Bob Hope

I once tried to smuggle my Pekingese past customs by wrapping him in my cloak. Everything was going splendidly until my bosom barked.

Beatrice Campbell

I've got a miniature poodle. The minute you're about to turn it does a poodle.

Jackie Gleason

I sometimes wonder if other dogs think poodles are members of some weird religious cult.

Rita Rudner

Only one thing really annoys me: tartan coats on small dogs.

Mitchell Symons

Last year for my birthday I was given a puppy. It's half poodle, half pit bull. Not a very good attack dog but a vicious gossip.

Bob Smith

'What would you get if you crossed a Rotweiler with a hyena?' 'I'm not sure, but if it laughs, I'll join in!'

Internet joke

My dog is half Labrador, half pit bull. She bites off my leg and then brings it back to me.

Frank Carson

Some dogs are pointers. Mine is a nudger. He's too polite to point.

Henny Youngman

An Airedale, erect beside the chauffeur of a Rolls-Royce, often gives you the impression he's there from choice.

E.B. White

My Dalmatian likes his drink. Last night I gave him a martini and he said, 'That hit the spot.'

Jackie Mason

What's black and white and red all over? A Dalmatian with sunburn.

Maureen Lipman

It was so hot out today I saw a Dalmatian with his spots on the ground.

Pat McCormick

I spilt spot remover on my dog. Now he's gone.

Steven Wright

Old Dogs and New Tricks

The only fault I can find with dogs is that they don't live to be a hundred.

Lewis Carey

Every healthy, normal boy should own a dog at some time in his life – preferably between the ages of 45 and 50.

Robert Benchley

I taught my dog to beg. Last night he came home with $11.

Sid Caesar

I brought my dog to Liverpool when I moved from Barcelona. He only took two days to learn Scouse. I still can't.

Luis Garcia

If Darwin was right, my dog would have learned to operate the can-opener by now.

Ricky Gervais

Try training your dog the way America trains its kids. Give the puppy her own set of house keys and put her in front of the television instead of taking her for a walk. Let her eat anything she wants and house-train herself. Send her to another master for visitation at the weekends. And when she comes into heat, turn her loose in the pound.

P.J. O'Rourke

I can train any dog in five minutes. It's training the owner that's the problem.

Barbara Woodhouse

If you can't teach an old dog new tricks, maybe you need a new dog.

Big O

My dog needed training so I brought him into the bedroom. From me he learned to beg. My wife taught him how to roll over and play dead.

Rodney Dangerfield

Growing Old

Actress years are like dog years. That makes me about 266.

Sharon Stone

I gave my youth to men. I'm going to give my old age to dogs.

Brigitte Bardot

The definition of old age? Realising you will never own all the dogs you wanted to.

Joe Gores

A friend of mine owned a dog. His 'roll over and play dead' routine was so realistic that when he eventually expired they had to get a second opinion so he could be buried.

Ronnie Corbett

I'll never forget my youth. I was a teacher's pet. She couldn't afford a dog.

Rodney Dangerfield

Sometimes it's fun to sit in your garden and try to remember your dog's name.

Steve Martin

A study I read said owning a dog can make you ten years younger. I was going to buy one but then I thought: Do I really want to go through the menopause again?

Joan Rivers

Biting the Hand that Feeds...

Percy was the dog's name. His guiding rule in life was, 'If it moves, bite it.'

P.G. Wodehouse

If you pick up a starving dog he will not bite you. This is the principal difference between a dog and a man.

Kinky Friedman

I said to my neighbour, 'Your dog bit me on the ankle.' He said, 'Come on, you don't expect a little dog like that to be able to reach up to your neck, do you?'

Les Dawson

Dogs never bite me, just humans.

Marilyn Monroe

For many of us, particularly myself, a dog is a set of sharp teeth mounted on four legs.

Robert Morley

My dog's been eating garlic. His bark is worse than his bite.

Paul Malone

I loathe people who keep dogs. They're cowards who haven't got the guts to bite people themselves.

Sir Geoffrey Streatfield

What a dog I have. His favourite bone is my arm.

Rodney Dangerfield

Dogs love their friends and bite their enemies, unlike people. People always mix love and hate.

Sigmund Freud

The noblest of all dogs is the hot dog. It feeds the hand that bites it.

Laurence J. Peter

Pavlov taught his dog to eat when he heard a bell. Two weeks later he savaged the postman.

Bob Monkhouse

When I worked for Securicor I was more scared of the guard dogs than the burglars.

Chris Tarrant

I'm opposed to the testing of dog food on animals.

Emo Phillips

A dog will never forget the crumb you gave him even if afterwards you throw a hundred stones at his head.

Saki

I believe they have eating dogs for anorexics now.

Duke of Edinburgh

Dog for sale. Eats Anything. Is particularly fond of children.

Newspaper ad

We asked for a square meals and guess what we got? Dog biscuits.

John Marshall

Did you ever consider how dogs see us? We come back from the grocery store with the most amazing haul – chicken, pork, half a cow. They must think we're the greatest hunters on earth.

Anne Tyler

My dog ate *Of Mice and Men* but was unable to finish *Moby Dick*.

George Steinbeck

My dog is worried about the fact that food has gone up by £1 a can. That's £7 in dog money.

Milton Berle

Dogs who earn their living by appearing on television commercials in which they constantly demand meat should remember that in at least one Far Eastern country they *are* meat.

Fran Lebowitz

A recipe is a series of step-by-step instructions for preparing ingredients you forgot to buy and utensils you don't own to make a dish the dog won't eat the rest of.

Henry Beard

Dogs on the Move

Dogs feel very strongly that they should always go with you in the car in case the need should arise for them to bark violently at nothing – right in your ear.

Dave Barry

Our dog is usually all right in the car but lately he's been getting bored. He's learned to push the horn button with his nose.

Alan Ayckbourn

Have you ever noticed that when you blow in a dog's face he gets mad but when you take him out in a car the first thing he does is put his head out the window?

Steven Wright

They say dogs know when storms are coming. I believe it. The last time we had one, our Alsatian got into the Buick and drove us to Nevada.

Bob Hope

My dog is so lazy he doesn't bother chasing cars. He just sits on the kerb taking down licence plate numbers.

Rodney Dangerfield

Don't take your dog on a space shuttle. If he sticks his head out when you're coming home he might burn up.

Jack Handey

A dog in the home is basically just a piece of moving furniture.

Philippe de Rothschild

Raining Cats and Dogs

You should be careful when it rains cats and dogs – you might step into a poodle.

Janet Rogers

Cats hate dogs because they care about people.

Peter Ford

A dog thinks: 'The people I live with feed me and love me, therefore they must be gods.' A cat thinks: 'The people I live with feed me and love me, therefore I must be a god.'

Louis Safian

What's the main difference between cats and dogs? Dogs have owners. Cats have staff.

Fay Weldon

A dog is a man's best friend. A cat is a cat's best friend.

Robert Vogel

A cat is a pygmy lion that loves mice, hates dogs and patronises human beings.

Oliver Herford

I'm not a cat man but a dog man. All felines can tell this at a glance – a sharp, vindictive glance.

James Thurber

If a dog jumps onto your lap it's because he's fond of you. If a cat does it's because your lap is warm.

A.N. Whitehead

Dogs come when they're called. Cats take messages and get back to you.

Mary Bly

A dog will sit beside you while you work. A cat will sit on the work.

Pam Brown

If animals could speak, the dog would be a blundering, outspoken honest fellow. The cat would have the rare grace of never saying a word too much.

Philip Hamerton

Robert Graves was fond of saying that he bred show dogs in order to be able to afford a cat.

Alastair Reid

Women and Children First

Children are for people who can't have dogs.

Victoria Wood

Bud Abbott loves his wife and he's got three dogs. I don't love mine and I've got two children. Go figure.

Lou Costello

Anyone who hates dogs and babies can't be all bad.

W.C. Fields

Anyone can have one kid but going from one to two is like going from owning a dog to running a zoo.

P.J. O'Rourke

My husband and I are either going to buy a dog or have a child. We can't decide whether to ruin our carpet or our lives.

Rita Rudner

My husband and myself don't have children. We've begun to long for the pitter-patter of little feet so we bought a dog. Well it's cheaper. And you get more feet.

Rita Rudner

Women who can't bear to be separated from their pet dogs often send their children to boarding schools quite cheerfully.

George Bernard Shaw

I bought a book about euthanasia for a woman I know who owns a dog. She said she couldn't put it down.

Frank Skinner

Winning is everything. The only ones who remember you when you come second are your wife and your dog.

Damon Hill

According to my children there are a lot of reasons I had them. One is that I needed someone around the house to eat the leftovers the dog wouldn't touch.

Erma Bombeck

The other night I had a fight with the dog and my wife took his side in front of him. Now he has no respect for me. She throws the ball, he waits for me to bring it back.

Rodney Dangerfield

Dogs are preferable to wives. The licence is cheaper and they already have fur coats.

Bob Monkhouse

I'm starting to feel a bit sorry for myself these days. My wife kisses our dog on the lips but she won't drink from my glass.

Rodney Dangerfield

My dog is just like one of the family. I won't say which one.

Bob Hope

The reason dogs are better than wives is because they never nag, never ask you to wash the dishes, and most of all they have no in-laws.

Fred Allen

My mom was a ventriloquist and was always throwing her voice. For ten years I thought it was the dog that was telling me to kill our father.

Wendy Liebman

Letting your child choose his bedroom furniture is like letting your dog choose his own vet.

Fran Lebowitz

When your first baby drops its soother you sterilise it. When your second one does so, you tell the dog, 'Fetch!'

Bruce Lansky

The honeymoon is over when the dog brings you your slippers and your wife barks at you.

Hugh Griffith

Women and cats will do just as they please. It's up to men and dogs to get used to the idea.

Robert Heinlen

We had to get rid of the kids. One of the dogs was allergic to them.

Annie Lewis

I'm the same with dogs as I am with daughters. They can have anything they want.

Orson Welles

That's Showbiz!

Like a fur accessory, Paris Hilton has a different dog to match every outfit.

Emma Jane Power

Showbusiness is worse than dog eat dog. It's dog won't return other dog's phone calls.

Woody Allen

Some of my best leading men have been dogs and horses.

Elizabeth Taylor

If a film of mine wasn't going well I always put a dog into it. It worked every time.

Walt Disney

Making a film with Marilyn Monroe was like directing *Lassie*. It took fourteen takes to get a print.

Otto Preminger

The first thing I do every day when I wake up is kiss my four dogs, all of whom sleep on top of me.

Liz Hurley

In order to feel safer in his private jet, John Travolta has purchased a bomb-sniffing dog. What a pity it came six movies too late.

Jay Leno

Winning an Oscar didn't change my life much. It didn't make my dog put out the bins for me, or do the housework.

Charlize Theron

I began to get worried about my film career when I realised I was second to Rin Tin Tin at the box office.

Judy Garland

My career and my family don't mix. It's like having two dogs that hate each other and you have to take them for a separate walk every night.

Tom Waits

Dogs are powerful in Hollywood today. No actor has ever won an Oscar playing opposite a dog – especially a dog with a trainer, an agent and a mobile phone.

Charles Grodin

Hollywood ain't dog eat dog. It's man eat man.

Wilson Mizner

I've been on so many blind dates I should get a free dog.
Wendy Liebman

It's fatal to let any dog know he's funny. He immediately loses his head and starts hamming it up.
P.G. Wodehouse

My mom took me to a dog show. And I won.
Phyllis Diller

The most memorable Father's Day present I ever got was a pair of slippers with rabbits' ears on them. Our dog is old and his sight isn't good. He thought they were two rabbits attacking me. He ate them while they were still on my feet.

Bill Cosby

Arnold Schwarzenegger's mother-in-law gave him a Labrador as a wedding present. She told her daughter to watch the way he treated the dog because that's the way he'd treat his kids. A couple of years later he ran over the dog.

Jack Dee

My career is like a dog. Sometimes it comes over when you call. Sometimes it gets up on your lap. Sometimes it rolls over. Sometimes it just won't do anything.

Tom Waits

I'd prefer one of my dogs to win a prize at Crufts than to have a Number 1 record.

Billy Mackenzie

When Maria Callas sang, she hit notes so high that only dogs could hear them. As far as I'm concerned, that was the dog's problem.

Bernard Manning

Bob Dylan's voice sounds like a dog with his leg caught in barbed wire.

Mitch Layne

I could never bring myself to vote for Margaret Thatcher. She spoke in the kind of voice that was telling you your dog had just died.

Keith Waterhouse

Love Me, Love My Dog

Love me, love my dog. But love me first.

Fred Allen

A dog is the only thing on earth that loves you more than you love yourself.

Josh Billings

Dogs are loyal, to be sure, but only to men, not to other dogs.

Karl Kraus

Henry Fonda had all the characteristics of a dog except loyalty.

Gore Vidal

Dog Fights

I'm very, very afraid of dogs, even nice dogs. Most dog-owners simply insist I haven't met the right dog yet.

Marian Keyes

The world is divided into those who can stop dog fights and those who cannot.

P.G. Wodehouse

It's not the size of the dog in the fight that counts but the fight in the dog.

Barry McGuigan

Intelligence

Dogs aren't that bright. Every time you come home they think it's amazing. You walk in the door and the joy of it almost kills them. 'It's that guy again! How does he do it?'

Jerry Seinfeld

No matter what you say to a dog, he gives you a look that says, 'My God, you're right. I never would have thought of that!'

Dave Barry

Our dog was the only intelligent member of the family. They say he was poisoned but nobody will convince me it wasn't suicide.

Hugh Leonard

Cats are smarter than dogs. You won't find eight cats pulling a sled through snow.

Jeff Valdez

The dog has seldom been successful in pulling man up to its level of sagacity but man has frequently dragged the dog down to his.

James Thurber

A Canadian psychologist is selling a video that teaches you how to test your dog's IQ. Here's how it works. If you spend $12 on the video, your dog is smarter than you are.

Jay Leno

My dog had very little Latin but had, as a pup, devoured Shakespeare. In a tasty leather binding.

Henny Youngman

Jimmy was showing off his 'genius' dog to his friend Mitch. 'This dog,' he beamed, 'is so clever he can even play gin rummy.' Mitch looked on amazed as Jimmy took a deck of cards out of his pocket. Sure enough, Rover proceeded to shuffle the pack and deal the cards. The two men sat down to play. After a few minutes, Mitch stood up. 'I thought you said that dog was clever,' he said. 'What's your problem?' Jimmy asked. 'He's useless,' Mitch insisted. 'Any idiot would have known the Three of Hearts was the card to play there instead of the Queen of Spades.'

Cormac O'Toole

Dogs would make incompetent criminals. If you could get a group of them to understand the concept of the Kennedy assassination, they'd all immediately confess to it.

Dave Barry

My dog is a magician. He's a Labracadabracador.

Fred Allen

Good Boy!

Dogs like to obey. It gives them security.

James Herriot

Most dog owners worry about obedience tests but do at length succeed in teaching themselves how to obey their dog.

Robert Morley

A boy can learn a lot from a dog: obedience, loyalty, and the importance of turning around three times before lying down.

Robert Benchley

I sent my dog to obedience school. He still bites me but now he says grace first.

Henny Youngman

British dogs are so well behaved they form orderly queues of one.

Mike Barry

'Let sleeping dogs lie' is an excellent maxim – unless you're stronger than the dog.

Hilda Lawrence

Party Poopers

My dog brings toilet paper to parties. He's a party pooper.

Jackie Mason

Dogs are the leaders of the planet. Imagine how it would look to an alien. You see two life forms. One of them has just done a poop. The other is carrying it for him. Who would you assume is in charge?

Jerry Seinfeld

Dogs only do their business when they know everyone is watching their owner. They want to know what to do with a pooper scooper.

John Sweeney

The reason there are no dogs on the moon is because there are no trees up there that they can pee against.

Dave Allen

My father used to hate it when dogs soiled our garden. He threatened to put up a sign saying, 'Dogs: Beware of Owner.'

Phelim Drew

I don't have a large garden. What I'm looking for is a dog with constipation.

Anette Helmsley

Some people have surprise birthday parties for their dogs. That's such a waste because any party would be a surprise for a dog.

Ellen DeGeneres

The other day I saw two dogs walking over to a parking meter. One of them said to the other, 'How do you like that? Pay toilets.'

Dave Starr

Puppy Love

One symptom of puppy love is when the boy dogs the girl's footsteps.

John Crosbie

Be wary of puppy love. It can lead to a dog's life.

Gladiola Montana

There's no psychiatrist in the world like a puppy licking your face.

Ben Williams

Watchdogs and Working Dogs

I got my grandmother a Seeing Eye dog but unfortunately he's sadistic. He does impressions of cars screeching to a halt.

Larry Amoros

I asked this woman why she had two Seeing Eye dogs. She said one was for reading.

Jonathan Katz

My dog can read. When he saw a sign saying, 'Wet Paint', he did.

Shaun Connors

If you send your dog to fetch the paper, make sure it knows which one to get. And don't give it too much money or it may not come back.

Mike Harding

Our watchdog doesn't bark. I usually let him sleep where burglars will fall over him and wake the rest of us.

Les Dawson

My brother has a great watchdog. He sleeps most of the day but anytime my brother hears a suspicious noise he wakes him up so he can start barking.

Henny Youngman

I wish scientists would come up with a way to make dogs bigger but with smaller heads. That way they'd still be good as watchdogs but they wouldn't eat as much.

Jack Handey

Watchdogs go tick woof, tick woof, tick woof.

Ronnie Barker

Dogs have a nice life. You never see a dog with a wristwatch.

George Carlin

I've named my dogs Rolex and Timex. They're watchdogs.

Pat Spillane

My dog works for the fire department. He helps locate hydrants.

Jackie Mason

My dog is timid. He's so afraid of burglars I had to put an alarm in his kennel.

Sid Caesar

I saw a sign outside a hospital, 'Guard Dogs Operating'. And I thought: Have the cutbacks got that bad?

Les Dawson

And now here are the results of the Sheepdog Trials. All the sheepdogs were found not guilty.

Keith Waterhouse

Walkies and Talkies

If it wasn't for dogs, people would never go for a walk.

Spike Milligan

I prefer to take my pet lobster for a walk than a dog. He doesn't bark.

Gerard de Nerval

A dog is an intelligent 4-footed animal who walks around with some dope on a leash.

Will Rogers

Dogs, like horses, are quadruped. That is to say, they have four rupeds, one at each corner, on which they walk.

Frank Muir

Every day my dog and I go for a tramp in the woods. He loves it, but the tramp is getting a bit fed up.

Jerry Dennis

[Hunting] I don't see why I should break my neck because a dog chooses to run after a nasty smell.

Arthur J. Balfour

I don't take my dog for a jog. He takes me.

Henny Youngman

It's untrue to say my dog can talk. If he says he can he's a bloomin' liar.

Jack Fennell

If dogs could talk, perhaps we would find it as hard to get along with them as we do with people.

Karel Capek

Why is it always the dog out for a walk who finds the dead body in TV programmes?

Simon Whaley

Tall Tails

You know you're drinking too much coffee when your
dog starts chasing his tail ... and you help him.

Lili Tomlin

The reason dogs have so many friends is because they
wag their tails instead of their tongues.

Carol Burnett

Where would a dog go if his tail fell off? The re-tail
store.

Fred Allen

A dog wags his tail with his heart.

Martin Buxbaum

Don't give out to your dog if he chases his tail. He's
only trying to make ends meet.

Frank Carson

If you're a dog and your owner suggests you wear a
sweater, suggest that he wear a tail.

Erma Bombeck

Every dog has his day but only those with broken tails have weak ends.

Nigel Rees

Why do dogs wag their tails? Because no one else will do it for them.

Janet Rogers

My granny wore a hearing aid that she kept at low volume. Whenever she turned it up it whistled and every dog in Dublin rushed to her side.

Terry Wogan

Dogs laugh with their tails.

Max Eastman

Well I'll Be Doggone

I lost my dog so I put an ad in the paper. Wasn't sure how to word it so I just wrote, 'Here, boy!'

Frank Carson

I saw this ad in a Boston newspaper: 'For sale, two female Boston terrier puppies, seven weeks old. Ring 55-1234. Leave mess.'

Carl Bremner

A man put an ad in the *Cork Examiner* for a lost dog. When it came time to pay the bill he refused. 'That dog doesn't even read the *Examiner*,' he insisted. 'He came back of his own free will.'

Niall Toibin

I saw this notice in a newspaper. 'Lost: Wife And Dog. Reward For Dog.'

Jeff Nielson

A Dog Walks into a Bar...

A dog goes into a bar and orders a martini. When the barman gives it to him he sits at the counter drinking it. The barman says, 'In all my years I've never seen anything like that.' The dog says, 'At these prices I'm not surprised.'

Sid Caesar

If you play a Country & Western song backwards, does that mean you go off the drink, your wife calls off the divorce and your dog comes back to life?

Gerald Hanley

Did you hear about the flea who won the lottery? He bought a dog in Marbella!

Ray Bates

These two fleas were too lazy to walk home ... so they took a dog.

Colin Ferris

A man walked into a psychiatrist's office. He said, 'Doctor, please help me, I think I'm a dog. The doctor told him to sit on the couch and they'd talk about it. 'I can't,' he said, 'I'm not allowed.'

Philip Adams

Did you hear about the dog who went to the flea circus?
He stole the show.

Jack Cruise

I wrote an essay on my dog for the teacher. He told me
it was exactly the same as my brother's. 'Of course it is,'
I explained, 'it's the same dog.'

Greg Sommers

Why did the dog with three legs walk into the saloon?
To find out who shot his paw.

Maureen Potter

What would you call a dog who made a bolt for the door? A blacksmith.

P.J. Coates

Patient: 'Doctor, doctor, I think I'm a dog.' Doctor: 'When did this start?' Patient: 'When I was a pup.'

Marsha Coates

What's the difference between a businessman and a hot dog? The businessman wears a suit but the hot dog just pants.

Don Rickles

What's black and white and looks good on a lawyer? A Doberman.

Mordecai Richler

A Scotsman bought a black-and-white dog because he thought the licence would be cheaper than for a coloured one.

Chubby Brown

What would you call a zoo without a dog? A shitzu.

Brian Belo

Why aren't dogs good dancers? Because they have two left feet.

Michael Cullen

A man took his dog to the vet because he kept getting sick. He vet took him up in his arms.

'I'm going to have to put him down,' he said.

'Why?' said the man, 'because he keeps getting sick?'

'No,' said the vet, 'because he's very heavy.'

Tommy Cooper

Two drunks were about to board a train when they saw a sign saying, 'Dogs Must Be Carried.'

'Hold it,' one says to the other. 'Where are we going to get a dog at this time of night?'

George Coote

I used to know this dog that sat in front of the TV set whenever there was rugby on. Every time Wales beat England at Cardiff Arms Park he used to jump in the air and bark out the score. Frank Bough from the BBC got to hear about it and came down to do a report.

'What does he do when England win?' he asked the dog's owner.

'I don't know,' he replied. 'We've only had him fourteen years.'

Max Boyce

'Dorothy, do you think I'm dressed okay for the dog races?'

'That depends. Are you competing?'

The Golden Girls

I saw a sign that said, 'Don't Let Your Dog Worry Wild Life.' And I thought: How is he going to do that? By going up to a bird and saying, 'Hey, I think you've got something on your back. It could be a tumour.'

Andy Kindler

Odds & Ends

Why are Arsenal players not allowed dogs? Because they can't hold a lead.

Jim Davidson

The reason dogs have no money is because they have no pockets. They see change on the street all the time and it drives them crazy.

Jerry Seinfeld

Watching a baby being born is a bit like watching a wet St Bernard coming in through the cat flap.

Jeff Foxworthy

Bonnie Prince Charlie was the only man ever to be named after three sheepdogs.

John Ross

My dog is not a piano substitute. At least that's what his piano teacher says.

Rita Rudner

Sign in a vet's office: 'Back in Ten Minutes. Sit!'

Joe McNamara

I didn't think I was ugly until the day my dog died from licking my wedding picture.

Phyllis Diller

It's not the end of the world that I lost my Olympic title. My dog will still lick my face.

Swimmer Matt Biondi in 1992

Asking a writer what he thinks about critics is like asking a lamp-post what it thinks about dogs.

Christopher Hampton

I bought a lap dog once but it didn't work out. Every time I sat on his lap he bit me.

Tommy Cooper

Never stand between a dog and a fire hydrant.

John Peers

Personally I don't see why a man can't have a dog or a girl. But if you can only afford one of them, get a dog.

Groucho Marx

I bought a dog so I could hear what's happening locally. Dog people are notorious gossips.

Jenny Éclair

I love dogs because they never hold grudges. They forgive you for everything – unless you get them wet.

Brendan Gleeson

Bill was a hard dog to keep on the porch.

Hillary Clinton

My husband has the face of a saint. A St. Bernard.

Roseanne

If you think you have influence, try ordering someone else's dog around.

Josh Billings

When a dog runs at you, whistle for him.

Henry David Thoreau

America is a large friendly dog in a very small room. Every time it wags its tail it knocks over a chair.

Arnold Toynbee

Asthma doesn't seem to bother me any more unless I'm around cigars or dogs. The thing that would bother me most would be a dog smoking a cigar.

Steve Allen

We're told Mother Hubbard went to the cupboard to get her poor dog a bone. I say Mother Hubbard had gin in there.

Jackie Mabley

My dog has a sore throat but I'm not worried about it. He's just a little husky.

Phyllis Diller

The only weights I lift are my dogs.

Olivia Newton-John

They say a reasonable amount of fleas is good for a dog. They keep him from brooding over the fact that he's a dog.

Edward Westcott

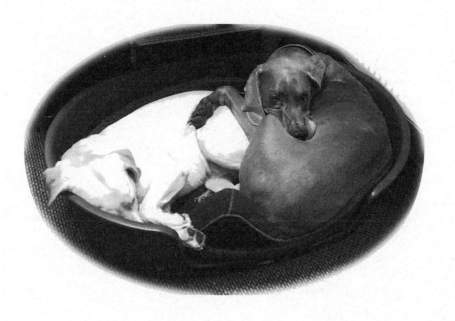

Also available from Barzipan Publishing
www.barzipan.com

Diana: I'm Going to be Me

Phil Dampier

ISBN: 978-0-992613-39-6

Price: £8.95

112 pp Paperback

Diana: I'm Going to be Me tells the remarkable story of Princess Diana's life through her own words. It is now 20 years since this iconic figure died at the tragically young age of 36 in a Paris car crash. In this first ever comprehensive collection of Diana's most memorable quotes, veteran royal reporter Phil Dampier reveals the heart and soul of an incredible woman who is missed by millions around the world. From the Queen's love of corgis and life as a Royal to love, fashion and mental health, this book reveals Diana's multiple facets. So sit back and celebrate the amazing life of this never-to-be forgotten woman – the beautiful, beguiling, flawed but uniquely enchanting Diana.

Prince Philip: A Lifetime of Wit and Wisdom

Phil Dampier and Ashley Walton

Cartoons by Richard Jolley

ISBN: 978-0-9926133-3-4

Price: £8.95

128pp Paperback

With delicious disregard for public opinion, the Duke of Edinburgh's acerbic comments and faux pas have provided feisty fodder for cartoonists and columnists for more than six decades. Seasoned royal correspondents Phil Dampier and Ashley Walton present an affectionate portrait of an extraordinary figure who in the last century was in many ways ahead of his time, but today is seen as the last Prince of political incorrectness.

Prince Philip: Wise Words and Golden Gaffes

Phil Dampier & Ashley Walton

Cartoons by Richard Jolley

ISBN 978-0-9573792-2-0

Price: £8.95

112 pp Paperback

His Royal Highness Prince Philip, the Duke of Edinburgh: irascible, controversial, outspoken, forthright and funny; the Gaffer, the Prince of Political Incorrectness, the Duke of Hazard, Phil the Greek. Whatever you call him – and he doesn't give a damn – you've got to love him. Now in his nineties, on he goes, undaunted, unrepentant and, if a little slower, just as amusing.

This book is a celebration of the wit and wisdom of a man whose unique style, down-to-earth humour and no-nonsense approach have brought colour into our lives. With delicious disregard for public opinion, his quips and faux pas have provided fodder for cartoonists and columnists for decades, and his one-liners are globally famous. With everything from frustrated beards and bloody great mechanical copulators to a bit of French bashing (and that ghastly place Stoke), this book will have you laughing out loud.

Cartoons for Grown-ups

Welcome to Yellowberry Hill!
A world much like ours ... only furrier

Mark Mowforth

ISBN 978-1-9997633-3-6

Price: £6.99

64 pp Paperback

Welcome to Yellowberry Hill, a bizarre and wonderful world of anthropomorphic animals just trying to deal with the with the challenges of daily adult life. With characters varying from a cat that owns a pet dog, to a quite small panda with attention deficiency and an unhealthy appetite for junk food, we are presented with hilarious wit and puns that will make you roll your eyes in amusement.

Naturally engaging, *Welcome to Yellowberry Hill!* is perfect for those who enjoy the quirky and unique...

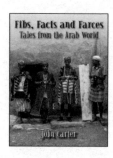

Fibs, Facts and Farces: Tales from the Arab World

John Carter

ISBN: 978-0-9570233-4-5

Price: £9.95

288 pp Paperback

The recent history of the Arab World presents a dismal story of pain, horror, and suffering. The causes are many and the blame game endless. However, the happy experiences of one Englishman throw a quite contrary light on current events, and have been written down as a way of saying thank you to all the Arabians involved for their unrivalled hospitality and friendship, as well as for sharing so much hilarious merriment.. The author has collected stories over the course of many years that highlight not only the essential dottiness of his own country's activities in the area, but also unveil the tremendous humour that the Arabs themselves possess.

"Formal history sometimes misses the humour, the misunderstandings and the flashes of insight to be found in stray correspondence, reported asides and the situation comedy inherent whenever cultures meet. John Carter lays out a rich store." — Matthew Parris

Anywhere but Saudi Arabia! Experiences of a (Once) Reluctant Expat

Kathy Cuddihy

ISBN: 978-0-9567081-3-7

Price: £9.95

308 pp Paperback

When Bechtel offered Sean Cuddihy a transfer to Riyadh, Saudi Arabia in 1976, his wife Kathy agreed to go along on one condition: that it was only for two years, not a minute longer. This reluctant commitment turned into a 24-year love affair with Saudi Arabia and its people. This book is a treasure for all who know and love the Kingdom, and an eye-opener for those with no comprehension of what life was, and is, like for an unconventional non-Muslim woman in a conservative Muslim population.